An opinionated guide to

NEW YORK ARCHITECTURE

Written by
ALLISON C. MEIER

Solomon R. Guggenheim Museum (no.53)

INFORMATION IS DEAD. LONG LIVE OPINION.

Who needs a guidebook when everything can be googled for free or found on ChatGPT? Because in an increasingly virtual world, you want lively, trustworthy *human* opinion.

This book is an unapologetically opinionated guide to the most brilliant buildings in NY – the ones you simply must see. We're an independent from east London. What business do we have writing a book about New York architecture? Quite a lot, actually. We're not slaves to Brutalism or servants of modernism. We don't care what's fashionable, and we're not snobs about what's 'too touristy'. We just love New York and are fanatical about design and culture.

If you told us you wanted to see, touch – and, dare we say it, smell – the city's most astonishing architecture, these are the places we'd send you.

Ann & Martin, co-founders
Hoxton Mini Press

Manhattan skyline

Brooklyn Bridge (no.65)

Opposite: Spring Street Salt Shed (no.23)

Sugar Hill Development (no.57)
Opposite: 41 Cooper Square (no.8)

A CITY THAT BELONGS
TO DREAMERS

There's an iron fence that circles Bowling Green, a small park in the Financial District. If you run your hand over the tops of its posts, you can feel rough, uneven surfaces. According to historical lore, royal finials – by some accounts crowns – were sawn off on 9 July 1776, in the revolutionary fervour following the Declaration of Independence.

It's a powerful thing to be able to touch a fence vandalised in the spirit of freedom in the 18th century. Noticing these details, especially in a city as dense as New York, reveals not just how the place has changed but who has transformed it. So many people have left their mark, whether influential individuals such as Robert Moses who ringed the city in expressways, or the immigrant communities who built sanctuaries in a new home. Even Broadway, the spine that runs down Manhattan, is said to have originated as an Indigenous trail, the memory of those footsteps embedded in its concrete path.

I moved to New York in 2009. Originally from a small town in Oklahoma, I found the congested blocks of the urban canyons both overwhelming and awe-inspiring. I walked endlessly in those early years – and still do, although with less tireless energy – and collected those details. I tried to find the oldest manhole covers, several marked as part of the Croton Aqueduct, which made its entrance to Manhattan on the triumphant arches of The High Bridge (no.62). I spent time in the cemeteries like Green-Wood (no.67) in Brooklyn, so fascinated by its soaring Gothic arch that I became a tour guide there.

I came to admire the city's brashness, how this archipelago of islands has used the strong bedrock of Manhattan to build one of the most varied and impressive skylines in the world. (The author Kurt Vonnegut wryly anointed it 'Skyscraper National Park'.) I also have, like anyone who stays here long enough, mourned what gets lost in that momentum. That's what makes it so remarkable that places like Brooklyn's Wyckoff House (no.68), the oldest structure not only in the city but the state, survive through the persistence of people who care for them.

Each of the sites in this book reflects someone's ambition to change the city, to add their vision to its story. I hope you're inspired to look more closely at the architectural icons and appreciate lesser-known locales, or better yet, get close enough to touch their steel, glass, granite and concrete that hold that history.

Allison C. Meier
New York, 2026

Allison C. Meier is a Brooklyn-based writer focused on the ways that design and culture shape our world. She moonlights as a cemetery tour guide and is the author of the book *Grave* (Bloomsbury, 2023) and several NYC architecture maps for Blue Crow Media.

GLOSSARY

*Explaining a few of the dominant styles shaping
New York's architectural landscape*

Dutch Colonial. Dutch colonists in the mid-17th century brought with them the steep roofs and stone walls of the architecture of the Netherlands. Historic survivors include the Dyckman Farmhouse (no.59) and Wyckoff House (no.68).

Neoclassical. Symmetry and order reign in this borrowing of the grandeur of ancient Greece and Rome. References to temples and civic monuments include columns, domes and colonnades, where marble abounds. See Gould Memorial Library (no.61) and the David N. Dinkins Municipal Building (no.18).

Beaux-Arts. Sharing a taste for antiquity with Neoclassical, Beaux-Arts is more opulent, with Italian Renaissance and Baroque touches. The New York Public Library (no.38) and Grand Central Terminal (no.37) demonstrate how the style, named for the École des Beaux-Arts in Paris, marked the Gilded Age.

Art Deco. The city soared in the 1920s and '30s, and Art Deco gave its skyscrapers and civic spaces, like Rockefeller Center (no.45), a jazzy edge, with embellishments and geometric forms. Modern materials were used to celebrate new technology, as demonstrated by the Chrysler Building (no.30).

Gothic. Pointed arches, ribbed vaults and stained glass defined European cathedrals in the Middle Ages. In the 19th century, Gothic Revival, or neo-Gothic, referenced this heritage in secular structures like the Jefferson Market Library (no.11) and the Woolworth Building (no.10).

Modernism. This global cultural movement rejected the ornamentation of the past for simpler, functional designs, elevating materials and form over decoration. It began its influence in NYC in the early decades of the 20th century, with pinnacles such as the Solomon R. Guggenheim Museum (no.53) and Lincoln Center (no.50).

International Style. After World War II, this was the dominant flavour of modernism, with its emphasis on flat surfaces and minimalism. Lever House (no.29) and the Seagram Building (no.42) are early examples of its unadorned rectilinear structures that remade the city's skyline in glass and steel.

Brutalism. A brasher mode of modernism that emerged in the 1950s, Brutalism took the emphasis on stark forms to the extreme. Its expressive shapes, made with exposed concrete, as seen in the Tracey Towers (no.60) and the Breuer Building (no.55), remain divisive.

Postmodernism. In the 1970s and '80s, a fatigue with boxy modernism led to an embrace of colour and detail. As seen in buildings like 550 Madison Avenue (no.48), postmodernism was whimsical and even provocative, with its nods to both history and pop culture and a rejection of austerity.

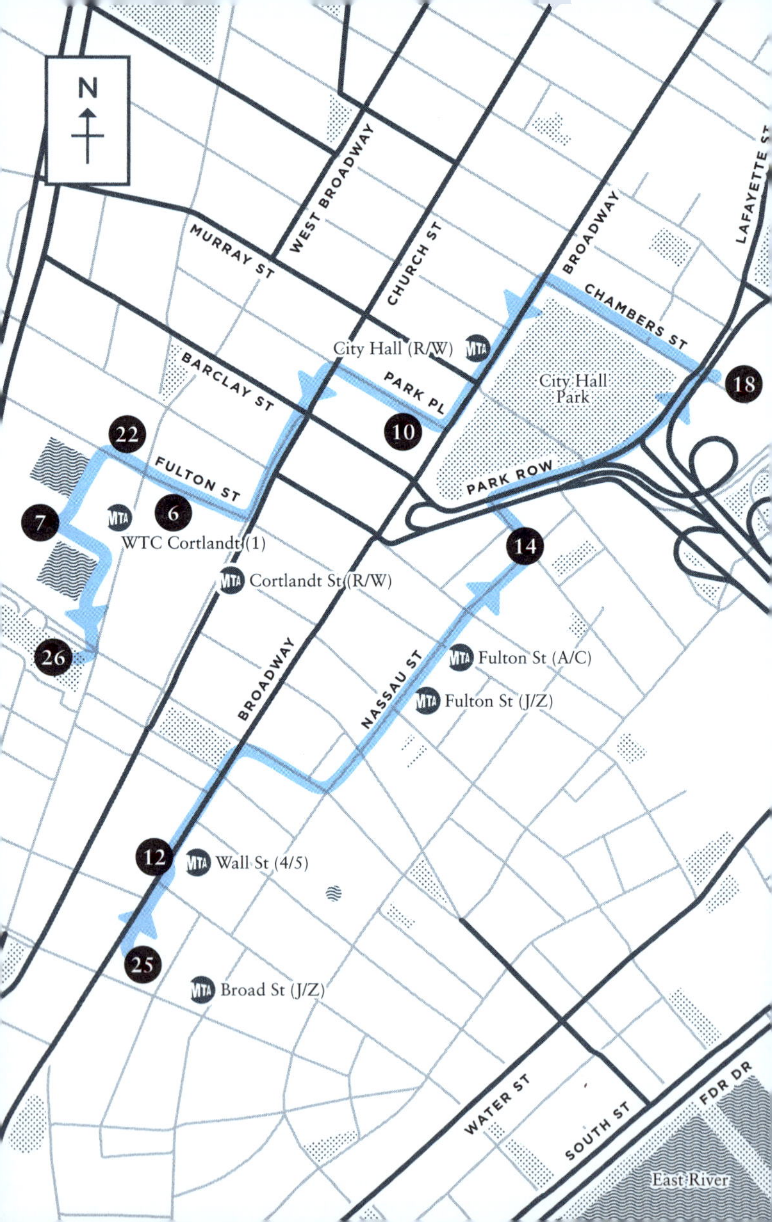

N
MURRAY ST
WEST BROADWAY
CHURCH ST
BROADWAY
CHAMBERS ST
LAFAYETTE ST
PARK PL
City Hall (R/W)
MTA
City Hall Park
18
BARCLAY ST
10
22
FULTON ST
PARK ROW
7
MTA
6
WTC Cortlandt (1)
14
MTA Cortlandt St (R/W)
BROADWAY
NASSAU ST
MTA Fulton St (A/C)
26
MTA Fulton St (J/Z)
12
MTA Wall St (4/5)
25
MTA Broad St (J/Z)
WATER ST
SOUTH ST
FDR DR
East River

WALK: LOWER MANHATTAN

Witness remembrance and revival across historic sites

Treat yourself to a coffee beneath the green-tented ceiling of Cafe Jalu at Printemps in One Wall Street **25** and take in the stunning mosaics of its Red Room. You are now ready to venture across centuries of history in what was colonial New Amsterdam. Memorials to past New Yorkers are in the graveyard outside Trinity Church **12**; spot the cryptogram on James Leeson's 1794 headstone, which deciphers to 'Remember Death'. Head up Broadway, turn right and then left onto Nassau Street until you hit Beekman, where you can discover the Romanesque Revival style of 5 Beekman Street **14**. Continue west and loop around City Hall Park to observe how the architecture evolves, including the Classical flair of the David N. Dinkins Municipal Building **18** and the neo-Gothic refinement of the Woolworth Building **10**. Back on Broadway, cut across Park Place to Church Street and head south to Fulton. Here you can see how Lower Manhattan rebounded following the 9/11 attacks. Cut through the Oculus **6**, then get up close to the marble cube of the Perelman **22** before entering the National 9/11 Memorial site **7**; seek out the small Callery pear tree that was rescued from the rubble. End with quiet contemplation in the luminous Saint Nicholas Church **26**.

Length: 2 miles
Walking time without stops: 40 minutes
Start: One Wall Street

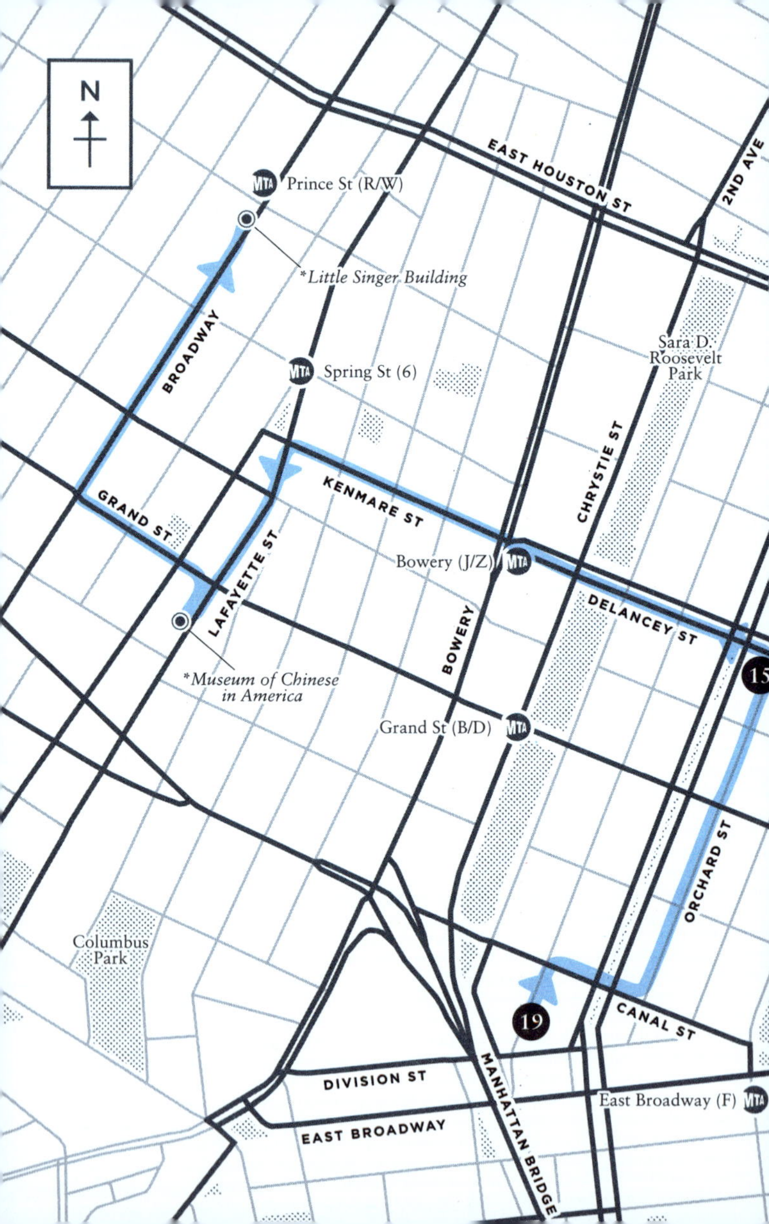

N
Prince St (R/W)
*Little Singer Building
EAST HOUSTON ST
2ND AVE
Sara D. Roosevelt Park
BROADWAY
Spring St (6)
CHRYSTIE ST
KENMARE ST
Bowery (J/Z)
DELANCEY ST
GRAND ST
LAFAYETTE ST
*Museum of Chinese in America
BOWERY
15
Grand St (B/D)
Columbus Park
ORCHARD ST
19
CANAL ST
DIVISION ST
East Broadway (F)
MANHATTAN BRIDGE
EAST BROADWAY

WALK: LOWER EAST SIDE

Discover grit and grace in a city of immigrants

The Lower East Side is where many immigrants' New York stories began. At the Museum at Eldridge Street Synagogue **19**, you can see where the pine floorboards have swayed imprints from the Eastern European Jewish congregation that prayed here. Continue north to the Tenement Museum **15** and take one of its informative tours through meticulously recreated apartments of 19th- and 20th-century immigrants. Head west and stop in the *Museum of Chinese in America**, where a permanent exhibition chronicles over 160 years of Chinese American history. Then make your way to SoHo–Cast Iron Historic District (no.13), where many immigrants worked in the manufacturing warehouses that sprang up in the 19th century behind ornate cast-iron facades, such as the *Little Singer Building** sewing machine factory. Notice how many sidewalks are embedded with glass, allowing light into subterranean factories that supported commercial ventures above. You can still find plaques from the local foundries that produced many of the metal building designs, recalling when industry and the people who made it all called this area home.

Length: 1 mile
Walking time without stops: 35 minutes
Start: Eldridge Street Synagogue
** Not in guidebook: more info online*

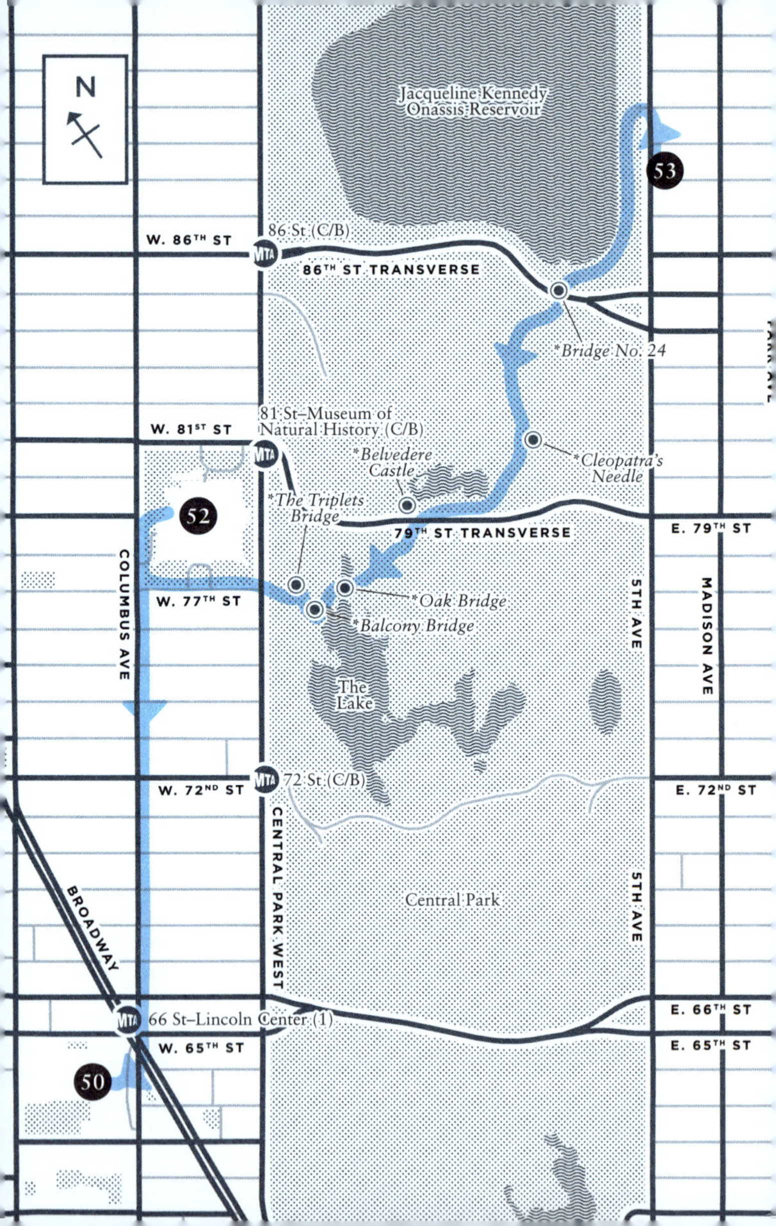

N
Jacqueline Kennedy Onassis Reservoir
53
W. 86TH ST
86 St (C/B)
86TH ST TRANSVERSE
*Bridge No. 24
81 St–Museum of Natural History (C/B)
W. 81ST ST
*Belvedere Castle
*Cleopatra's Needle
52
*The Triplets Bridge
79TH ST TRANSVERSE
E. 79TH ST
W. 77TH ST
*Oak Bridge
*Balcony Bridge
COLUMBUS AVE
The Lake
5TH AVE
MADISON AVE
72 St (C/B)
W. 72ND ST
E. 72ND ST
CENTRAL PARK WEST
BROADWAY
Central Park
5TH AVE
E. 66TH ST
66 St–Lincoln Center (1)
W. 65TH ST
E. 65TH ST
50

WALK: CENTRAL PARK

Get cultured in New York's green heart

This tour takes you to three cultural hubs, so check their calendars for what's happening to make the most of your journey. The first stop is the Solomon R. Guggenheim Museum **53**. Although curators usually start their exhibitions at ground level, Frank Lloyd Wright intended visitors to take the elevator to the atrium's top and descend its spiralling ramp. Don't exhaust yourself, as Central Park is across the street with many arches and bridges (no.51) to navigate. Pass over the lacy cast-iron *Bridge No. 24** alongside the reservoir and cut down East Drive, taking in *Cleopatra's Needle**, an obelisk dating to 1425 BCE transported here in the 1880s. Walk the trail south of Turtle Pond, below the fairy-tale *Belvedere Castle**, and explore the rustic atmosphere of *Oak Bridge**, *Balcony Bridge** and *The Triplets Bridge**, until you're back out in busy Manhattan at Central Park West. If you're ready for another museum pit stop, the Gilder Center's **52** concrete canyon at the American Museum of Natural History is here, or you can head south to the modernist Lincoln Center **50** to catch a show.

Length: 3 miles
Walking time without stops: 1 hour
Start: Solomon R. Guggenheim Museum
** Not in guidebook: more info online*

N
8TH AVE
7TH AVE
BROADWAY
6TH AVE
5TH AVE
MADISON AVE
PARK AVE
LEXINGTON AVE
3RD AVE
2ND AVE
W. 53RD ST
W. 50TH ST
W. 49TH ST
W. 46TH ST
W. 45TH ST
W. 42ND ST
W. 37TH ST
W. 34TH ST
E. 50TH ST
E. 42ND ST
E. 37TH ST
E. 34TH ST
E. 31ST ST
E. 30TH ST
PARK AVE TUNNEL
39
45
47–50 St–
Rockefeller Center
(B/D/F/M)
*Bryant Park
5 Av (7)
43
38
37
30
31
33 St (6)
MTA
MTA
MTA

4

WALK: ART DECO MIDTOWN

Be awed by the city's Jazz Age icons

Art Deco redefined Manhattan's skyline, adding its tallest skyscrapers to date. Begin with the victor of this race: the Empire State Building **31**. Tours are available to the top, but for free, you can crane your neck to its jazzy setbacks. Take 34th east to Lexington and go north until 42nd: here is its elegant competitor, the auto-inspired Chrysler Building **30**. You'll get a better perspective as you go west on 42nd (check the time on the ornate Tiffany glass clock adorning Grand Central Terminal **37** as you go by); look back at Fifth Avenue to take in its curved crown. Walk south past the Beaux-Arts New York Public Library **38** and make a right on 40th to the American Radiator Building **43**, a dramatic neo-Gothic statement in gold and black. Grab a seat in *Bryant Park** to take in the view, or continue north on Sixth Avenue to 50th. Radio City Music Hall **39** beckons; notice roundels by Hildreth Meière of performers on the facade. Take a tour, or stroll into Rockefeller Center **45**, where you could spend hours discovering its details, from the statue of Atlas carrying the weight of the world to Josep Maria Sert's sprawling *American Progress* mural.

Length: 2 miles
Walking time without stops: 50 minutes
Start: Empire State Building
* Not in guidebook: more info online

N
MTA 5 Av/53 St (E/F)
29
42
MTA Lexington Av/53 St (E/F)
MTA 51 St (6)
E. 57TH ST
E. 54TH ST
E. 53RD ST
E. 50TH ST
E. 49TH ST
E. 46TH ST
E. 45TH ST
E. 42ND ST
5TH AVE
MADISON AVE
PARK AVE
LEXINGTON AVE
3RD AVE
2ND AVE
1ST AVE
FDR DR
37
36
*MetLife Building
*The United Nations
East River

5

WALK: MID-CENTURY MIDTOWN

Meet the maestros of modernist design

The post-World War II enthusiasm for clean lines and refined materials informed what became known as mid-century modernism. You can see architecture by its influential progenitors in New York, some of whom had fled the rise of fascism in Europe, such as Bauhaus founder Walter Gropius, who worked on the former Pan Am Building (now the *MetLife Building**) that looms over Grand Central Terminal ㉟. Start at that transport nexus like a true commuter and head north on Park Avenue. At the corner of 53rd, Mies van der Rohe's Seagram Building ㊷ and Gordon Bunshaft and Natalie de Blois's Lever House ㉙ face off with two gleaming versions of glass corporate boxes. Continue east to First Avenue and turn south. The *United Nations complex** emerges on your left. The glass slab of the Secretariat contrasts with the low swoop of the General Assembly, a fusion of the distinctive visions of modernity by Oscar Niemeyer and Le Corbusier. Finally, rest your feet in the public atrium of the Ford Foundation ㊱, where lush foliage softens the metal and glass to create a tranquil harmony.

Length: 2 miles
Walking time without stops: 40 minutes
Start: Grand Central Terminal
** Not in guidebook: more info online*

6

OCULUS

Phoenix from the ashes

A dove flying out of a hand is what Santiago Cala-trava envisioned in the gargantuan spikes rising from this transportation hub. Part of the World Trade Center site reconstruction, its central sky-light is aligned with the sun's angles to cast a beam timed to the anniversary of the 9/11 attacks, illuminating two symbolic columns of light on the floor below. Its swooping ribbed form provokes awe and frustration from the commuters who nav-igate its maze-like marble halls. And then there is its staggering $4 billion cost, making it one of the world's most expensive train stations. Enter and look up through the colossal curving steel to catch a glimpse of the sky in a ribbon of glass. Decide for yourself if it's an uplifting civic statement or a monstrous money pit.

50 Church Street, New York, NY 10007
Nearest subway: WTC Cortlandt (1)
Access: Open to the public; limited access overnight
explorewtc.com

Santiago Calatrava (2016)

THE MILLENIUM HILTON

7

ONE WORLD TRADE CENTER & 9/11 MEMORIAL

On absence

Rebuilding after the destruction of the World Trade Center required reconciling with the void left by the terrorist attacks. The new complex attempts to heal, remember and move forwards. The memorial landscape itself is minimal but meditative, with waterfalls cascading into the footprints of the missing towers, wounds that will never entirely mend. Underground, the museum preserves artefacts of those lost structures, from a massive slurry wall to a battered staircase. And soaring above it all is One World Trade Center, the tallest building in the country. It may not yet have the instant recognisability of the Twin Towers, but it declares, in its ambitious height, the city's resilience.

One World Trade Center: 285 Fulton Street,
New York, NY 10007;
Memorial: 180 Greenwich Street, New York, NY 10007
Nearest subway: WTC Cortlandt (1)
Access: Open daily to the public
onewtc.com, 911memorial.org

One World Trade Center: SOM (2014)

9/11 Memorial: Michael Arad and Peter Walker (2011)

8

41 COOPER SQUARE

Armoured in steel against its critics

When Cooper Union's Foundation Building opened in 1859, it included a cylindrical shaft because inventor and industrialist Peter Cooper believed building elevators would soon exist, even if they didn't yet. When the college later made its expansion across the street, it was similarly futuristic. Draped in perforated metal to shield it from the sun, this tough-skinned building has weathered local criticism for looking so alien in the East Village and from alumni for its hefty cost. As more area developments have risen in sterile glass and steel, Morphosis founder Thom Mayne's design of a sci-fi academic building still makes a statement. Look through the street-level windows to see its ethereal core: a skylit 20-foot-wide, four-storey-tall staircase.

41 Cooper Square, New York, NY 10003
Nearest subway: Astor Place (6)
Access: Accessible on campus tours
cooper.edu

Morphosis Architects (2009)

9

WHITNEY MUSEUM OF AMERICAN ART

Industrial chic in the Meatpacking District

The Whitney's previous home on Madison Avenue by Marcel Breuer (no.55) is rugged granite and concrete; this new building glints with glass and steel. It's not the masterwork that the 1966 building is, yet where Breuer focused the museum inwards, here the city is on show. As with Renzo Piano's Pompidou in Paris, exposed mechanical systems are joined by external staircases and terraces that look out to The High Line (no.35). To feel like a real art insider, find Lawrence Weiner's manhole cover in the sidewalk outside, and a lobby flagstone reading 'It Always Seems Impossible Until It's Done'. That's where a work by Maurizio Cattelan (the Italian artist behind such provocations as a solid gold toilet formerly installed in the Guggenheim) was reinterred from the old museum.

99 Gansevoort Street, New York, NY 10014
Nearest subway: 14th Street/Eighth Avenue (A/C/E/L)
Access: Ticketed entry
whitney.org

Renzo Piano Building Workshop (2015)

10

WOOLWORTH BUILDING

Built by nickels and dimes

When this neo-Gothic skyscraper claimed the world's tallest building crown (held until 1929), it was such an event that President Woodrow Wilson pressed a button from the White House to illuminate its lights. These new heights were reached through a 792-foot steel frame supported by caissons, a process in which metal tubes were pneumatically driven into the exceptionally deep bedrock beneath this part of Manhattan. It was dubbed the 'Cathedral of Commerce' for its terracotta flourishes, barrel-vaulted ceilings and ornamental sculpture. The public is often sternly turned away from the lobby, but if you make it in, look for grotesques of architect Gilbert holding a building model and his patron, F. W. Woolworth (of five-and-dime fortune), counting coins.

233 Broadway, New York, NY 10279
Nearest subway: Park Place (2/3)
Access: Closed to the public, view from the street
woolworthbuilding.com

Cass Gilbert (1913)

11

JEFFERSON MARKET LIBRARY

Follow the spiral stairs to a court of reading

In the 1950s, before NYC's 1965 landmarks law, community members rallied to save this High Victorian Gothic former courthouse from the wrecking ball. Abandoned and in disrepair, it was reimagined as one of NYC's most attractive libraries by architect Giorgio Cavaglieri. Long before adaptive reuse of historic structures became standard, he thoughtfully updated its design for readers. A vivacious polychrome mix of materials, including red and black brick, granite, sandstone trim and a slate roof, culminates at a fire lookout tower. A civil court with stained-glass windows became the main reading room; the more spartan basement prisoner holding area was turned into a quiet reference room. Don't miss the garden next door, one of the neighbourhood's havens of calm.

425 Avenue of the Americas, New York, NY 10011
Nearest subway: Christopher Street–Stonewall (1)
Access: Open to the public
nypl.org/locations/jefferson-market

Frederick Clarke Withers of Vaux and Withers (1877); Giorgio Cavaglieri (1967)

12

TRINITY CHURCH

Manhattan's spiritual soul for 300 years

Wall Street ends at a churchyard, its tombs with winged skulls and hourglasses dating back to the 17th century, affirming that all mortal wealth is fleeting. Nevertheless, the Financial District has flourished skywards around it in the centuries that this Episcopal parish has worshipped on the site. This is the third of its churches, built in a Gothic Revival style from the brownstone used throughout NYC architecture. In the nave, it forms pointed arches, with trompe l'œil painting making the plaster walls appear like matching bricks. The public is welcome to visit for reflection here or among the graves where departed New Yorkers, including Alexander Hamilton, are remembered.

89 Broadway, New York, NY 10006
Nearest subway: Wall Street (4/5)
Access: Open to the public daily
trinitychurchnyc.org

Richard Upjohn (1846)

13
SOHO–CAST IRON HISTORIC DISTRICT

Manhattan's most metal neighbourhood

There are around 250 cast-iron buildings in NYC, most of which are in SoHo, making it the largest collection in the world. Cast-iron facades, predominantly dating from the middle to late 19th century, were an American innovation. Cheaper than stone or brick and able to reinforce taller structures, cast iron could be mass-produced for an expanding industrial zone. After being threatened with destruction for the (thankfully unrealised) Lower Manhattan Expressway, this area was designated a historic district in 1973. Standouts include the iron filigree on the Little Singer Building's balconies, the E. V. Haughwout Building with its five-storey corner block that anticipated the frames of skyscrapers and the battleship grey 101 Spring Street, where artist Donald Judd had his studio.

Bordered by West Houston Street, Crosby Street,
Canal Street and West Broadway
Nearest subway: Prince Street (R/W)
Access: Most buildings private, view from the street

Judd Foundation, 101 Spring Street, Nicholas Whyte (1870)

14
5 BEEKMAN STREET

A buried treasure revealed

Cast-iron dragons support a jaw-dropping nine-storey atrium in this brick and terracotta building once known as Temple Court. From the outside, you can see its twin peaked towers that gave it what counted as skyscraper height in the late 19th century. Starting in the 1940s, the atrium was walled off for nearly 70 years as a fire hazard. It became a secret, a move that accidentally preserved it, until a restoration revealed its treasures. When it re-opened in 2016 as the Beekman, following the building's revival into apartments and hotels, it was one of the city's great architectural surprises. Grab a drink at the bar beneath its pyramidal skylight and let it take your breath away.

5 Beekman Street, New York, NY 10038
Nearest subway: Fulton Street (2/3/4/5/A/C/J/Z)
Access: Atrium open to the public
thebeekman.com

Silliman & Farnsworth (1883)

15

TENEMENT MUSEUM

How the other half lived

Most historic homes preserve the stories of the wealthy or famous; this museum concentrates on the immigrant and working-class experiences of ordinary people based on the 19th-century tenement at its heart. Its founders, historian Ruth Abram and artist Anita Jacobson, happened on the 1863 building at 97 Orchard Street in 1988 after it had been boarded up in 1935, leaving it untouched for more than 50 years. The pressed-metal ceilings, wooden staircase and layers of wallpaper left by generations of families from across the world were intact; further investigation revealed forgotten possessions beneath the floorboards. The building is a palimpsest still being decoded, each new discovery adding to the stories that it tells.

97 and 103 Orchard Street, New York, NY 10002
Nearest subway: Delancey Street/Essex Street (F/J/M/Z)
Access: Visit is by guided tour
tenement.org

Contracted by Lukas Glockner (1863)

16
WASHINGTON SQUARE ARCH

Honouring the country's first president

Stanford White was the starchitect of the Gilded Age, designing breathtaking Manhattan landmarks like Penn Station and the old Madison Square Garden, where he was dramatically murdered on its rooftop in 1906. Here, the flamboyant partner in McKim, Mead & White borrowed from Roman triumphal arches to venerate the great American hero, George Washington. For over six decades, traffic went under and around its carved marble. Now pedestrian-only as a gateway to Washington Square Park, its restored carvings of Washington's life and American history show off White's mastery of grand ornamentation. Step under the arch and look up to see 95 rosettes, each of their petals delicately hand-carved.

Washington Square Park, New York, NY 10012
Nearest subway: West Fourth Street–Washington
Square (A/C/E/B/D/F/M)
Access: Viewable in public park

Stanford White (1895)

17

BAYARD–CONDICT BUILDING

A modern master's only New York work

Louis Sullivan wrote that a skyscraper should be 'every inch a proud and soaring thing', and the Chicago architect's only NYC building is all about verticality. Only 12 storeys – still daring for the 19th century – it appears taller. Follow the long lines of its six vertical bays up to where they culminate in angels with wings spread beneath the cornice. Sullivan is considered the father of modern American architecture for how he eschewed emulating the Classical world and instead expressed the new. Ornament was used selectively, and while there's plenty here on the white terracotta curtain wall, it all serves to emphasise the upward lines of the steel frame below.

65 Bleecker Street, New York, NY 10012
Nearest subway: Bleecker Street (6)
Access: Closed to the public, view from the street

Louis Sullivan with Lyndon P. Smith (1899)

18

DAVID N. DINKINS MUNICIPAL BUILDING

A confection of Classical references

The 25-foot-tall gilded lady – decked out with symbols of the city – who stands on the central tower of this government building was based on Audrey Munson. Her modelling was so prolific she was nicknamed 'Miss Manhattan'. Her presence is just one of the reasons to look up and spot the details on one of the last statements of the City Beautiful movement, in which urban planning concentrated on monumental grandeur. This was the first Manhattan building to have a subway station in its base, a decade after the first station opened. When exiting, commuters emerge below an arcade of vaulted ceilings covered with the Guastavino tiles that embellish Beaux-Arts architecture across the city.

1 Centre Street, New York, NY 10007
Nearest subway: Chambers Street (J/Z)
Access: Closed to the public, view from the street

William M. Kendall of McKim, Mead & White (1914)

19

ELDRIDGE STREET SYNAGOGUE

Worn floorboards tracing generations of prayer

Today, Eldridge Street Synagogue is radiant, with its star-painted ceiling and zodiac mosaic floor. But imagine what it was like for its Eastern European Jewish immigrant community when it opened in 1887: their previous spaces for worship had been humble storefronts and event halls. This purpose-built home was proudly crowned with towers decorated with Stars of David, while the sanctuary within was adorned with Moorish and Gothic ornamentation. A decline that started in the 1920s with waning membership led to its abandonment, so it was claimed as a roost for pigeons until the 1980s. Following a painstaking 20-year, $20 million restoration, the building was revived as a museum, opening in 2007.

12 Eldridge Street, New York, NY 10002
Nearest subway: East Broadway (F)
Access: Paid entry during museum hours
eldridgestreet.org

Peter and Francis William Herter (1887)

20

SILVER TOWERS

1960s urban renewal done with class

I. M. Pei was still up-and-coming when he and James Ingo Freed worked on this 'superblock' – an urban planning approach to concentrating housing in a pedestrian area. It was known as University Village until two of its structures that serve as NYU housing were renamed Silver Towers in 1974. Pei was heavily inspired by reading about modernist architecture pioneer Le Corbusier's rejection of the ornamentation of earlier eras like Art Nouveau in favour of the use of simplified materials and form. While the three concrete towers here aren't as famous as Pei's later works like the Louvre Pyramid, they are well proportioned with each oriented in a slightly different way. Bringing it all together is Picasso's 36-foot-tall concrete *Bust of Sylvette* (fabricated by Carl Nesjar as Picasso never travelled to the United States) in the grassy plaza.

100 and 110 Bleecker Street, New York, NY 10012
Nearest subway: Broadway–Lafayette Street (B/D/F/M)
Access: Plaza open to the public

James Ingo Freed and I. M. Pei (1967)

21

NATIONAL MARITIME UNION BUILDING

A grounded ship in Greenwich Village

The scalloped edges of this building come together like a huge overbite. Few architects were as whimsical in their modernism as Albert C. Ledner, who gave a nautical flair to each of his designs for the National Maritime Union. This structure, with its white facade of portholes and an elevator bulkhead resembling a ship's chimney stack, is the most traffic-stopping of the three in New York. (The other two are now nearby hotels, also with circular windows.) It later became part of a hospital, which received permission to tear it down in 2008. Luckily, the plan didn't go ahead, and instead it was renovated into the Lenox Health Greenwich Village facility that opened in 2014.

30 Seventh Avenue, New York, NY 10011
Nearest subway: 14th Street (1/2/3)
Access: Closed to the public, view from the street
gvh.northwell.edu

Albert C. Ledner (1964)

22

PERELMAN PERFORMING ARTS CENTER

A beacon of light at Ground Zero

In the complicated, often contentious, rebuilding of the World Trade Center site, having a space for the arts was always part of the plan. It took decades to realise, with this cultural complex right across from the 9/11 Memorial (no.7) championing the city's undaunted creative spirit. It is relatively modest in size compared to its towering Lower Manhattan neighbours, but in a resourceful use of space, it packs three flexible venues into a 138-foot-tall cube that floats on a granite plinth. Most astonishing is its day-to-night transition, when its creamy exterior, made up of thousands of thin marble tiles, illuminates from within, creating an amber lantern patterned by the veined stone.

251 Fulton Street, New York, NY 10007
Nearest subway: WTC Cortlandt (1)
Access: Lobby open to the public; ticketed events
pacnyc.org

REX and Davis Brody Bond (2023)

23
SPRING STREET SALT SHED

Civic architecture as art

Why should a utilitarian building be bland? Most sheds that store salt for de-icing winter roads are workhorses, but this is a work of art. The craggy concrete structure was inspired by what it holds in heaps: a grain of salt. The side facing the Hudson River is peaked higher to match what is poetically known as the salt's 'angle of repose': the steepest angle at which a pile of salt can be formed without collapsing. By day, the shed is a photoshoot destination – possibly the first such honour for a Department of Sanitation building. Come by at night to witness how its crystalline edges are dramatically illuminated from below.

336 Spring Street, New York, NY 10013
Nearest subway: Spring Street (C/E)
Access: Closed to the public, view from the street

Dattner Architects with WXY Architecture + Urban Design (2015)

24
NEW MUSEUM

A daring design for fearless art

The Bowery was grittier than it is today when this off-kilter stack of seven blocks rose above the surrounding restaurant supply stores and a few of the old flophouses hanging on against gentrification. The aluminium-clad structure was an unconventional design for a museum that, since 1977, had challenged what an art institution could be, but had never had a permanent home. The Tokyo-based firm SANAA gave the New Museum a space that encapsulated its anti-establishment vibe, with the very simple, nearly windowless galleries immersing visitors in challenging and provocative exhibitions. A major expansion by international architectural firm OMA is planned to open in 2026 with a prismatic neighbour of complementary glass and metal mesh, doubling its exhibition space.

235 Bowery, New York, NY 10002
Nearest subway: Second Avenue (F)
Access: Ticketed entry for exhibitions
newmuseum.org

SANAA (2007)

25

ONE WALL STREET

A building with a heart of fire

Muralist Hildreth Meière gave many of the city's Art Deco buildings an incandescent touch, from colourful roundels on Radio City Music Hall (no.39) to an arch of Byzantine-style mosaics at Temple Emanu-El. At One Wall Street is her most fantastic interior, although, until its recent restoration, it was only known to serious design aficionados. Once the reception room for a major bank, the double-storey Red Room is ablaze with floor-to-ceiling mosaics of orange and red accented with gold. This fluted limestone skyscraper was converted into luxury condos in 2023, and from 2025 has had an outpost of the Paris department store Printemps, inviting the public in to experience the building's once obscure brilliance.

1 Wall Street, New York, NY 10005
Nearest subway: Wall Street (4/5)
Access: Retail levels open to the public
onewallstreet.com

Ralph Walker of Voorhees, Gmelin and Walker (1931)

26
SAINT NICHOLAS GREEK ORTHODOX CHURCH

A luminous resurrection

The small but dedicated congregation of Saint Nicholas Greek Orthodox Church worshipped in a former 19th-century tavern for almost a century. Then the collapse of the south tower of the World Trade Center on September 11, 2001, destroyed their community's home. Rebuilding took years as the challenge of construction in a place of so much loss took shape. Finally, a marble dome supported by four stone-clad towers was consecrated in 2022. Its architect, Santiago Calatrava, also designed the more ostentatious Oculus (no.6) at Ground Zero, with both displaying his preference for crisp white forms. Non-members are welcome to step inside for a quiet pause. Seeing the church at night is most poignant, when it softly glows from within.

130 Liberty Street, New York, NY 10006
Nearest subway: WTC Cortlandt (1)
Access: Open daily, 10am–5pm
stnicholaswtc.org

Santiago Calatrava (2022)

27
STATUE OF LIBERTY

Sentinel for freedom

Some sites are so familiar it's hard to consider them with fresh eyes, but imagine encountering this green giant for the first time, perhaps as an immigrant at the adjacent Ellis Island. What she embodies is a freedom that will not be stopped. She strides forwards over a broken chain, the torch in her hand triumphantly lifted to the sky. Hidden under her thin copper skin – oxidised by the harbour air – is a steel framework that allows her to sway with the wind, even enduring hurricanes that have battered the city. While nothing beats encountering her 305-foot height up close, the not-so-secret tip is that the free Staten Island Ferry offers views alongside.

Liberty Island, New York, NY 10004
Nearest subway: Whitehall Street–South Ferry (R/W)
Access: Visits operated by the National Park Service;
ticketed daily ferry service
nps.gov/stli/index.htm

*Sculpture: Frédéric Auguste Bartholdi; Framework: Gustave Eiffel;
Pedestal: Richard Morris Hunt (1886)*

28
HEARST TOWER

Dramatic reinvention of a media headquarters

This should be an abomination: a 21st-century glass protrusion erupting from a 1920s core. The original building was meant to be the base of a taller structure, but this was never realised. Finally, 80 years later, Norman Foster's crystalline tower of glistening glass and steel has manifested with a diagonal grid of triangles, sheathed by the shell of the flamboyant Art Deco building below. So often in New York, the architectural past is demolished to make way for the next thing. Preserving the facade creates a lively conversation between old and new, what design was and where it is going. This forward vision is visible inside as well: access the lobby to see the striking *Ice Falls*, where collected rainwater rushes over glass prisms to help cool and humidify the atrium.

300 West 57th Street, New York, NY 10019
Nearest subway: 59th Street–Columbus Circle (A/C/B/D)
Access: Public access limited to the entrance lobby
hearst.com/real-estate/hearst-tower

Joseph Urban and George B. Post & Sons (1928); Foster + Partners (2006)

29

LEVER HOUSE

Modernist masterpiece of corporate design

Every aspect of Lever House brings to mind a single word: clean. Fitting, given that the building was designed as the HQ of Lever Brothers soap company. The main tower, a sparkling curtain of blue-green glass, cascades over Park Avenue. Sleek, steel-clad columns hold the base aloft, inviting the public into its landscaped plaza – an unusual decision for an office building, not normally so welcoming. Glass boxes now crowd Manhattan, but this, built from 1950 to 1952, was the first. Its construction announced the arrival of the International Style from Europe, characterised by minimal forms and industrial materials. Look into the lobby and imagine its first visitors in an optimistic post-war era, before inelegant imitators cluttered the skyline.

390 Park Avenue, New York, NY 10022
Nearest subway: Fifth Avenue/53rd Street (E/F)
Access: Plaza, courtyard and lobby open to the public
leverhousenyc.com

Gordon Bunshaft and Natalie de Blois of
Skidmore, Owings & Merrill (SOM) (1952)

30

CHRYSLER BUILDING

Art Deco at its finest

The Chrysler Building pierces the clouds with a gleaming spire, bursting from its steel-clad sunburst crown. This element was covertly built within the skyscraper's frame and constructed in just 90 minutes so its architect could – albeit briefly – claim the title of the world's tallest building. Now surpassed in stature by newcomers on all sides, the building remains unrivalled in its Art Deco splendour. Funded by automotive titan Walter P. Chrysler, it is an unabashed celebration of the 20th-century car industry. Look closely to spot winged radiator caps adorning corners and metallic hood ornament-inspired eagle heads watching over the city from a roost on the 61st floor. Step into the red granite-lined lobby where a sprawling ceiling mural is dedicated to the human ingenuity of transportation.

405 Lexington Avenue, New York, NY 10174
Nearest subway: Grand Central–42nd Street (7)
Access: Lobby open to the public during building hours

William Van Alen (1930)

31

EMPIRE STATE BUILDING

Skyline icon where King Kong climbed

Notice how many New York City buildings resemble tiered wedding cakes? The 1916 Zoning Resolution required setbacks, so buildings got narrower as they got taller to keep the streets below from becoming a dark, airless abyss. The influence of these laws is especially striking on this Art Deco giant of the 1930s skyscraper boom. The Empire State Building elegantly tapers as it reaches 1,250 feet, where its mast was originally envisioned as an airship dock. That version of the future never arrived, but visit the spectacular lobby to see Jazz Age optimism preserved. Don't miss the dazzling metal mural of the building itself installed on the marble walls beneath a gold-leaf ceiling of stars.

20 West 34th Street, New York, NY 10001
Nearest subway: 34th Street–Herald Square
Access: Lobby open to the public during building hours;
ticketed entry to observation decks
esbnyc.com

Shreve, Lamb and Harmon (1931)

32

GENERAL ELECTRIC BUILDING

Crowned by the deities of radio

If there's a building to get binoculars out for, it's this, because at its crown, 640 feet in the sky, Art Deco pizzazz *really* goes wild. Electrical bolts shoot upwards around colossal figures whose heads radiate lightning. This cathedral-like Gothic grandeur glorifies not faith, but human ingenuity. It was built for the Radio Corporation of America (RCA) Victor, with all those zigzags and terracotta ornaments of electrical charges celebrating the technological power of the radio. When General Electric later took over, they barely had to change a thing: just a clock with their logo replaced one above a corner entrance surmounted by two metal hands grasping electric rays.

570 Lexington Avenue, New York, NY 10022
Nearest subway: 51st Street (6)
Access: Closed to the public, view from the street

Cross & Cross (1931)

33

HELMSLEY BUILDING

Honeycombed tower holding a vehicular corridor

Congestion at Grand Central would be pandemonium without this Beaux-Arts beauty that doubles as a traffic solution. Overshadowed now by the hulking 1963 MetLife Building (formerly the Pan Am Building), the Helmsley's grace likely goes unnoticed by those who speed under the archways that allow motorists to go through it rather than around it. It was initially built to be the headquarters of the New York Central Railroad and complements the station through a design by the same architects, with the railroad's initials recurring in its lustrous lobby. Still an office building, it has struggled in recent years with a high vacancy rate. Visit during the annual Summer Streets, when Park Avenue is limited to bikes and pedestrians, and you can walk through its portals usually reserved for cars.

230 Park Avenue, New York, NY 10169
Nearest subway: Grand Central–42nd Street (4/5/6/7/S)
Access: Closed to the public, view from the street
230parkavenue.com

Warren & Wetmore (1929)

THE HELMS

Y BUILDING

34
FLATIRON BUILDING

Looking sharp for 120 years

Some called this severely wedged building 'Burnham's Folly' when architect Daniel Burnham completed it in 1902, as they believed it would topple over in the wind. But history has been kind to this early skyscraper. Even before construction, the land here was nicknamed 'flatiron', as its shape resembled a clothes iron. That awkward plot, distinct from the surrounding gridded blocks, demanded a building suited to its slender proportions. Today, it's one of the most photographed buildings, captured by everyone from Alfred Stieglitz to Edward Steichen. Zoom in on its lavish terracotta, or step back to take in its form that cuts through the air like a ship's prow. A condo conversion underway will soon give the building exterior night-time lighting for the first time.

175 Fifth Avenue, New York, NY 10010
Nearest subway: 23rd Street (R/W)
Access: Closed to the public, view from the street
theflatironbuilding.com

Daniel Burnham (1902)

35

THE HIGH LINE

Elevated urban renewal

It's the adaptive reuse project that inspired cities around the world to rethink their own industrial relics. This disused 1930s railway track has been transformed into a 1.45-mile-long green haven suspended over the streets below. Revolutionary garden designer Piet Oudolf drew inspiration from the railway's self-seeded wilderness, cultivating a space that will grow and evolve over time. The linear park has, in some ways, been a victim of its own success, as luxury buildings increasingly block its view and crowds on summer days clog its narrow paths. Pick an off-peak time to experience The High Line at its best, when from this perch you can watch the flow of life that makes New York so magnetic.

Gansevoort Street to West 30th Street between Washington Street and Eleventh Avenue, New York, NY 10011
Nearest subway: 34th Street–Hudson Yards (7)
Access: Free entry, open daily
thehighline.org

James Corner Field Operations, Diller Scofidio + Renfro and Piet Oudolf (2009–23)

36

FORD FOUNDATION CENTER FOR SOCIAL JUSTICE

Escape Midtown in an urban jungle

Before green architecture became a trend, there was the Ford Foundation. Its roof collects rainwater and its expansive glass walls filter in natural light that illuminates its centrepiece: a 12-storey atrium flourishing with plants around a reflecting pool. The public is welcome into this lush botanical garden, where private offices overlook the urban oasis. Structural materials harmonise with the foliage, from the soaring columns of red granite to the window grids of rusted steel. Although some touches are 1960s time capsules – ashtrays are embedded in the vintage seating – the building remains as beguiling as when it debuted as a radical new vision of a corporate building, one in which you might actually like to linger.

320 East 43rd Street, New York, NY 10017
Nearest subway: Grand Central–42nd Street (7)
Access: Atrium garden and art gallery open to the public
fordfoundation.org

Kevin Roche John Dinkeloo and Associates with Dan Kiley (1967)

37
GRAND CENTRAL TERMINAL

New York's celestial station

Grand Central is such a beloved destination, it's hard to believe it was once threatened with demolition. Rail travel's decline and the station's deterioration – you can still see a pre-renovation patch on the ceiling where cigarette smoke and other grime once coated it – led to plans to bulldoze it and replace it with an office tower. Now, it's protected inside and out, from its vault of constellations over the main concourse to the statue of Mercury crowning its exterior. Many overlook the Beaux-Arts details that make it truly special, like the acorn motif (a symbol of the Vanderbilts who financed it), and its innovation in using accessible ramps rather than stairs. Go against the commuter currents and pause to marvel at this temple to transportation.

89 East 42nd Street, New York, NY 10017
Nearest subway: Grand Central–42nd Street (4/5/6/7/S)
Access: Open to the public during building hours
grandcentralterminal.com

Reed and Stem, Warren & Wetmore (1913)

Vanderbilt Ave
East 42nd St
PRIVATE EYES
GENTLEMEN'S CLUB
POLICE

38

NEW YORK PUBLIC LIBRARY

Marble monument to reading

Guarded by stone lions – named 'Patience' and 'Fortitude' in the 1930s by Mayor Fiorello La Guardia to represent endurance through the Great Depression – the New York Public Library's main branch is among the city's grandest structures. From Fifth Avenue, its Classical influences are evident in the marble portico of arches, statuary and fluted Corinthian columns. Inside, you'll find Beaux-Arts details – right down to the wastebaskets. Look down when crossing the bridge to the shop and cafe to see stone remnants of the 1842 reservoir that was here before and supplied the city's drinking water. And if you want to enjoy the Rose Reading Room's cloud-covered ceiling without taking a tour, bring a book and (quietly) say you're there to read.

476 Fifth Avenue, New York, NY 10018
Nearest subway: 42nd Street–Bryant Park/
Fifth Avenue (B/D/F/M/7)
Access: Open to the public, free tours
nypl.org

Carrère and Hastings (1911)

39

RADIO CITY MUSIC HALL

Rosy-fingered dawn takes the stage

Entering beneath the neon marquee with the name of this renowned music venue in red, blue and gold does not prepare you for the splendour within. While the limestone exterior elegantly matches the rest of Rockefeller Center, inside it glows with brass, chrome and aluminium. Rather than encrust the walls with decoration like other Art Deco buildings, interior designer Donald Deskey went for restraint in a streamlined aesthetic. This does not make its bold use of geometry and line any less impressive. At its heart is the theatre, the world's largest such indoor space when it opened, where stepped arches mimic the breaking dawn of a sunrise.

1260 Avenue of the Americas, New York, NY 10020
Nearest subway: 47th–50th Streets–
Rockefeller Center (B/D/F/M)
Access: Tours are available in addition to ticketed events
msg.com/radio-city-music-hall

Edward Durell Stone and Donald Deskey (1932)

40
HOTEL CHELSEA

Legendary for its bohemian past

Wrought-iron flowers flourish over the balconies of this fabled hotel, a motif that continues inside on its skylit staircase, upon which too many famed names to list have walked. (Dylan Thomas died there, Andy Warhol filmed there and Leonard Cohen immortalised it in song.) The neon sign on its 11 storeys of red brick, topped by a high, steeply sloped mansard roof with dormer windows, became an emblem of bohemian life. Those days are over: since 2022, it's been a renovated, far swankier hotel than when a creative enclave of tenants stayed long-term in its affordable rooms. Brass plaques galore border its lobby doors, recalling the music, literature and art that wouldn't exist without it.

222 West 23rd Street, New York, NY 10011
Nearest subway: 23rd Street (1)
Access: Open to Hotel Chelsea guests
and restaurant and bar patrons
hotelchelsea.com

Philip Hubert of Hubert, Pirsson & Company (1885)

41

THE MORGAN LIBRARY & MUSEUM

A bibliophile's dream

The original entrance to what started as banker J. P. Morgan's personal library on East 36th Street was inspired by the Villa Medici, with architect Charles McKim continuing the Italian Renaissance intricacy inside. Mosaics, murals and columns of lapis lazuli abound. A rotunda foyer ushers visitors into a glistening room of gold ceilings and floor-to-ceiling bookcases. Many of the rare books collected by Morgan are still on the shelves; keep an eye out for brass handles that hide doors to the upper levels. Although visitors now enter through the 2006 expansion by Renzo Piano – who also designed the new Whitney Museum (no.9) – the jewel of the complex remains this 'bookman's paradise', as one astonished visitor anointed it in 1908.

225 Madison Avenue, New York, NY 10016
Nearest subway: 33rd Street (6)
Access: Ticketed entry
themorgan.org

Charles McKim of McKim, Mead and White (1906)

42
SEAGRAM BUILDING

The reason every office tower is a glass box

As the Seagram Building is one of the 20th century's most imitated, it can be hard to appreciate its refinement amidst its mediocre copies. Commercial design has borrowed so heavily from Ludwig Mies van der Rohe that slabs of glass and metal dot every business district, yet these lack his subtle use of proportion and austere symmetry. While he's best known for his 'less is more' ethos, that 'less' was sumptuous. Luxurious bronze clads the exterior, the material continuing inside – designed with his acolyte Philip Johnson – where each doorknob and mail chute is custom. The pink-granite half-acre plaza is edged by green marble and embedded with two fountains, offering to the public what could be part of the architectural footprint.

375 Park Avenue, New York, NY 10152
Nearest subway: Lexington Avenue–53rd Street (E/F)
Access: Plaza is accessible to the public
seagram375park.com

Ludwig Mies van der Rohe, Philip Johnson, Kahn & Jacobs (1958)

43

AMERICAN RADIATOR BUILDING

An Art Deco beauty brings the heat

Raymond Hood thought too many buildings looked like a 'waffle stood on end' with their light masonry and dark windows. So instead, he made this Art Deco tower from moody black brick. Built for the American Radiator Company, this dark palette flickers with Gothic gold ornamentation by sculptor Rene Paul Chambellan. The grotesques were inspired by medieval art, but with a modern twist, such as a pipefitter holding a wrench. Night-time floodlighting of its roof suggested a glowing radiator, a surreal sight that inspired Georgia O'Keeffe to paint it from her window in 1927. Now a hotel, you can get a drink in the arched basement, which was once a showroom for furnaces and boilers.

40 West 40th Street, New York, NY 10018
Nearest subway: 42nd Street–Bryant Park (B/D/F/M)
Access: Accessible to Bryant Park Hotel guests
and restaurant and bar patrons
bryantparkhotel.com

Raymond Hood and André Fouilhoux (1924)

44

MODULIGHTOR BUILDING

A modernist take on the row house

Interlocking white I-beams make this building appear like a jigsaw puzzle. Paul Rudolph's buildings have sometimes been scorned for their complexity – his bold, seven-storey Yale Art and Architecture Building in Connecticut (now known as Rudolph Hall) somehow contains over 30 levels – but few architects have created such artful geometric forms. This is the building he designed for himself late in his career, and it doubles as a residential and commercial space for the lighting company he created with his partner, Ernst Wagner. Its duplex apartment is regularly opened to visitors by the institute dedicated to his legacy, and rather than treating it as a museum, the institute invites visitors to sit on the built-in furniture and interact with the space.

246 East 58th Street, New York, NY 10022
Nearest subway: 59th Street (4/5/6)
Access: Ticketed open houses held monthly
paulrudolph.institute

Paul Rudolph (1993)

45

ROCKEFELLER CENTER

Midtown's Art Deco jewel

In 1931, the first Christmas tree was decorated at Rockefeller Center by the Italian, Irish and Greek workers grateful for jobs during the hard years of the Great Depression. Now, the lighting of a huge tree in the plaza is the lodestar of NYC's holiday season; below it, ice skaters are watched over by Paul Manship's gilded *Prometheus* stealing fire for us mortals. Art Deco details in murals and sculpture can be found everywhere on the complex's 14 original limestone buildings, designed by a team of architects led by Raymond Hood and funded by philanthropist John D. Rockefeller Jr. Look for sculptor Gaston Lachaise's bas-relief at 45 Rockefeller Center honouring those workers who built this 'city within a city'.

45 Rockefeller Plaza, New York, NY 10111
Nearest subway: 47th–50th Streets–
Rockefeller Center (B/D/F/M)
Access: Plaza open to the public; ticketed tours available
rockefellercenter.com

Associated Architects (1939)

46

432 PARK AVENUE

Status symbol towers like a Lego stack

The area around Central Park's desirable southern edge increasingly resembles a pincushion. It's known as Billionaires' Row, as being able to live supertall means possessing super wealth. Several of these buildings fit the definition of 'pencil tower' for their reedy height, including this svelte structure that at 1,396 feet is the world's third-tallest residential building. It held the top spot until it was outranked by the nearby Central Park Tower and Steinway Tower (no.49). But its white lattice of concrete (inspired by the gridded pattern of a 1905 rubbish bin designed by Vienna Secession architect Josef Hoffmann) is in a precarious state: as of 2025, cracks had riddled its facade.

432 Park Avenue, New York, NY 10022
Nearest subway: Fifth Avenue/53rd Street (E/F)
Access: Closed to the public, view from the street
432parkavenue.com

Rafael Viñoly and SLCE Architects (2015)

47

FRANKLIN D. ROOSEVELT FOUR FREEDOMS PARK

Order, design and composition in harmony

It took almost four decades for this park on a landfill site to be realised after Louis Kahn designed it in 1974. Intended to honour the 32nd president, it is as much a tribute to the late architect who imbued its imposing granite blocks with a lightness of form. For Kahn, the structure and materials of architecture were specific and meaningful. Symmetry reigns. It was named for FDR's famed 1941 speech, in which he advocated for freedom of speech, freedom of worship, freedom from want and freedom from fear. Kahn created a space of meditation on these essential liberties. The emphasis is on stillness, on being conscious of your place among the lines of linden trees as you take in the views of the East River and the skyline beyond.

1 FDR Four Freedoms Park, Roosevelt Island, NY 10044
Nearest subway: Roosevelt Island (F/M)
Access: Open year-round, check hours online
fdrfourfreedomspark.org

Louis Kahn (1974); *completed* 2012

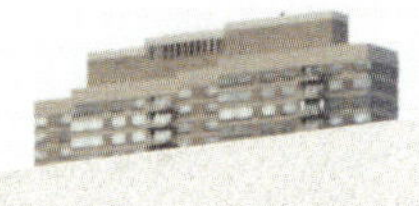

IN THE FUTURE DAYS WHICH WE SEEK TO MAKE SECURE,
WE LOOK FORWARD TO A WORLD FOUNDED UPON FOUR
ESSENTIAL HUMAN FREEDOMS. THE FIRST IS FREEDOM OF
SPEECH AND EXPRESSION - EVERYWHERE IN THE WORLD. THE
SECOND IS FREEDOM OF EVERY PERSON TO WORSHIP GOD
IN HIS OWN WAY - EVERYWHERE IN THE WORLD. THE THIRD
IS FREEDOM FROM WANT...EVERYWHERE IN THE WORLD.
THE FOURTH IS FREEDOM FROM FEAR...ANYWHERE IN THE
WORLD. THAT IS NO VISION OF A DISTANT MILLENNIUM.
IT IS A DEFINITE BASIS FOR A KIND OF WORLD ATTAINABLE
IN OUR OWN TIME AND GENERATION.
FRANKLIN D. ROOSEVELT
JANUARY 1941

48

550 MADISON AVENUE

The first postmodern skyscraper

Nothing else on the skyline looks like this playful reworking of Classical arches and arcades into one of the earliest major postmodernist works. With a choice of pink granite for the exterior, Philip Johnson declared that he was leaving modernism's asceticism behind. It's nicknamed the 'Chippendale' building for the way its pediment, broken with a round hole, resembles the English woodworker's furniture. However, the prevailing taste for slick glass and steel skyscrapers could not be stopped, and instead of signalling a new age, 550 Madison is a relic of 1980s optimism. An aggressive 2020s renovation by Snøhetta was scaled back after critical outcry, the resulting expanded public garden respectfully nodding to this past in its circular forms, providing a lush respite for New Yorkers.

550 Madison Avenue, New York, NY 10022
Nearest subway: Fifth Avenue/53rd Street (E/F)
Access: Garden open to the public
550madison.com

Philip Johnson and John Burgee (1984)

49

STEINWAY TOWER

Stairway to the clouds

The serrated setbacks of this supertall tower make it stand out from the other spindly ultra-luxury developments south of Central Park. Its steel crown slices the sky, looking like a staircase to the heavens. With a 1:24 width-to-height ratio, it is the world's skinniest skyscraper. It's technically an expansion using the air rights of the landmarked 1925 Steinway Hall far below, designed by Warren & Wetmore for the Steinway & Sons piano company. Both are now rarefied air for those who can afford their apartments; only they can say whether the sway of the 1,428-foot building that happens at such heights is worth it on the windiest days.

111 West 57th Street, New York, NY 10019
Nearest subway: 57th Street (F/M)
Access: Closed to the public, view from the street
111w57.com

SHoP Architects (2022)

50

LINCOLN CENTER FOR THE PERFORMING ARTS

Modernist cultural acropolis

New York has few plazas where pedestrians can gather without dodging traffic: Lincoln Center, with its circular fountain surrounded by the 1960s modernist colonnades of its many performance venues, is one of them. Yet the thriving San Juan Hill community was here before, with urban renewal plans displacing its residents to make way for the cultural complex. The elegance of its design by the superstars of mid-century architecture is undeniable, with white travertine marble-clad exteriors and plush interiors for opera, dance and music, but it has frequently felt like its own island. Expansions over the years have connected this ever-evolving arts campus more seamlessly to its neighbourhood.

Lincoln Center Plaza, New York, NY 10023
Nearest subway: 66th Street–Lincoln Center (1)
Access: Plaza open to the public, paid entry to tours
lincolncenter.org

Wallace Harrison, master plan; Max Abramovitz, Pietro Belluschi, Gordon Bunshaft, John Burgee, Philip Johnson, Dan Kiley, Eero Saarinen (1962–68)

51
THE ARCHES OF CENTRAL PARK

Stroll through Manhattan's iconic green space

The 36 arches and bridges that criss-cross Central Park are not just ornamental. Planners Frederick Law Olmsted and Calvert Vaux purposefully used these spans to separate pedestrian, horse rider and carriage traffic. Many of the current arches date back to the 1860s, and each has its own character, designed by Vaux to complement its natural setting. The brick and sandstone Willowdell Arch holds niches with benches for weary wanderers on the Mall; Pinebank Arch soars over a bridle path with a filigree of cast iron that contrasts with the craggy outcrops on either side. Most spectacular is Huddlestone Arch in the North Woods. Made with huge boulders that 'huddle' together without any mortar, the rustic stone archway appears as if it sprang up organically from the land itself.

Central Park, New York, NY
Nearest subway: 59th Street–Columbus Circle (A/C/B/D/1)
Access: Open daily, 6am–1am
centralparknyc.org

Bethesda Terrace, Calvert Vaux (1869)

52

GILDER CENTER

Concrete canyon of natural wonders

Most natural history museum architecture imposes order on nature; the latest expansion of the American Museum of Natural History celebrates its raw forces. The Gilder Center's atrium of porous concrete was inspired by how wind and water shape landscapes – natural light streams in through skylights over the walkways and curving portals. Visiting the space feels like exploring a cave or canyon, where discoveries include windows offering views into an insectarium, a storeroom containing millions of specimens and a room filled with free-flying butterflies. Curiosity is nurtured here, so don't be afraid to open the doors to the fourth-floor research library and see where the building's sinuous concrete becomes an arboreal canopy above this trove of knowledge.

200 Central Park West, New York, NY 10024
Nearest subway: 81st Street–Museum of
Natural History (A/B/C)
Access: Ticketed entry
amnh.org

Studio Gang (2023)

The Richard Gilder Center for Science, Education, and Innovation

53
SOLOMON R. GUGGENHEIM MUSEUM

Legendary American architect's final design

With its stack of sweeping curves a total contrast to its Upper East Side neighbours, Frank Lloyd Wright boasted that this museum would make the Met down the street 'look like a Protestant barn'. It's undeniable that a visitor to the Guggenheim probably thinks of its prickly architect more than the designers of most museums; you can even find his signature on a small red tile on the outside, a mark he embedded on the projects of which he was especially proud. And all art installed along the quarter-mile-long ramp must compete with the vistas from his circular rotunda, where the eye is constantly drawn away to gaze across the nautilus shell of coiling concrete or up to the natural light pouring through its oculus.

1071 Fifth Avenue, New York, NY 10128
Nearest subway: 86th Street (4/5/6)
Access: Ticketed entry
guggenheim.org

Frank Lloyd Wright (1959)

54

PARK AVENUE ARMORY

Gilded Age veteran to arts destination

This 19th-century armoury has come a long way since being named one of the world's most endangered historic sites in 2000. Restored, but with some atmospheric decay in situ, its 55,000-square-foot drill hall hosts experimental works that could only be realised in such an enormous venue, from an opera featuring a flock of 100 sheep to an installation of 42 swings. Its unsung gems are its historic rooms. When the Seventh Regiment erected the block-sized building, its prominent families, like the Roosevelts and Vanderbilts, enlisted designers including Louis Comfort Tiffany and the Herter Brothers. Mahogany woodwork, copper-leaf ceiling panels and wrought-iron grillwork recall its role as a social as well as a militaristic space.

643 Park Avenue, New York, NY 10065
Nearest subway: 68th Street–Hunter College (6)
Access: Ticketed tours are available in
addition to programming
armoryonpark.org

Charles W. Clinton (1881)

55

BREUER BUILDING

The colossus of Madison Avenue

When it opened in 1966, the Whitney Museum of American Art was derided by some critics as bunker-like and aggressively heavy for its bulky inverted ziggurat that hangs over Madison Avenue. Bauhaus-trained Marcel Breuer wanted it to stand out from the streetscape of office and residential buildings to emphasise 'the sincerity and profundity of art'. After taking in its sparse trapezoidal windows and mass of grey granite covering the cantilevered floors, cross the concrete bridge above the sunken courtyard, enter the galleries and immerse yourself in this landmark of modern architecture. Acquired by Sotheby's in 2023, it is now celebrated as a Brutalist masterpiece and remains one of New York's boldest spaces to view visual art.

945 Madison Avenue, New York, NY 10021
Nearest subway: 77th Street (6)
Access: Free entry, galleries are open to the public
sothebys.com/en/about/locations/new-york

Marcel Breuer & Associates (1966)

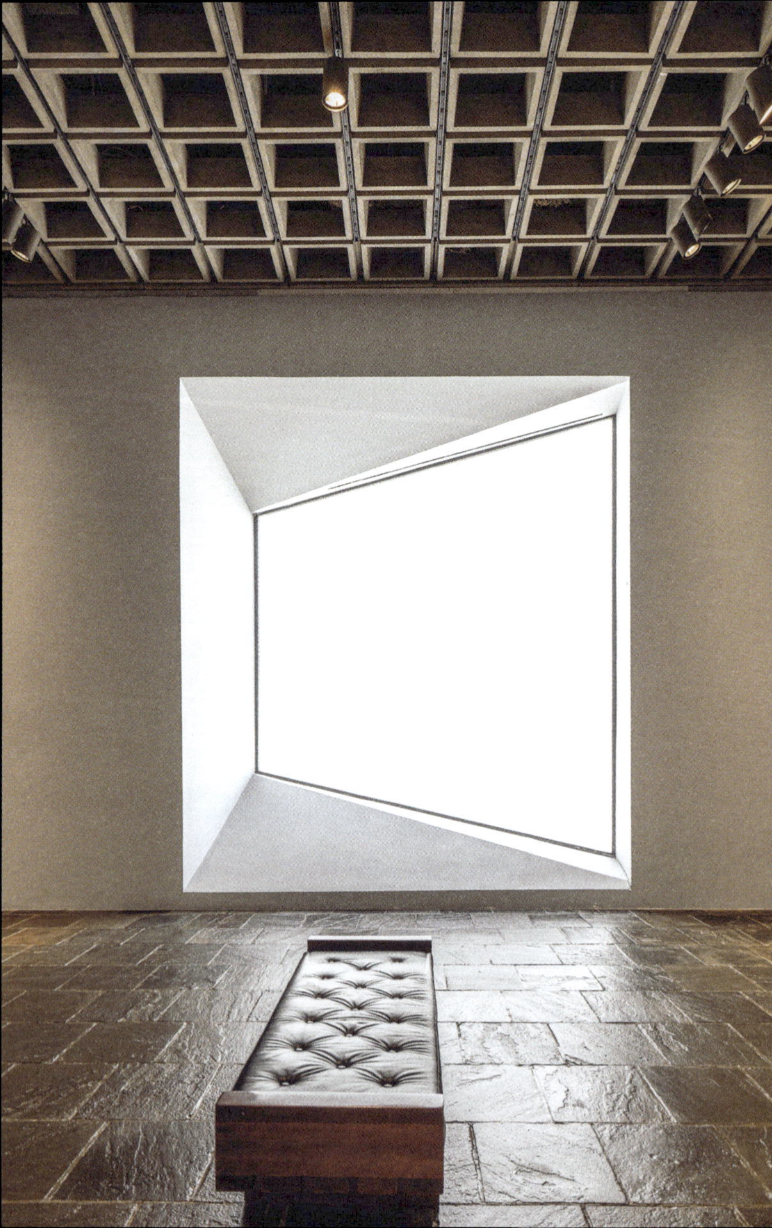

56

STUDIO MUSEUM IN HARLEM

A Black art champion's bold new home

In 1968, a group of artists, civic leaders and activists founded a museum to uplift artists of African descent who were marginalised in other institutions. Its earliest home was a rented loft. After decades of adapting existing architecture, this impactful place has a purpose-built home. It opened in November 2025 and is dynamic without dominating its Harlem block. The dark grey precast concrete framing its windows of varying sizes is softened with sandblasting and polishing in various textures. It promises to age better than exposed light grey concrete, which is so easily streaked with stains, and these differing forms reflect the vibrant mixing of exhibitions, residencies and programming within.

144 West 125th Street, New York, NY 10027
Nearest subway: 125th Street (2/3)
Access: Ticketed entry
studiomuseum.org

Adjaye Associates (2025)

57

SUGAR HILL DEVELOPMENT

A new type of affordable housing

Affordable housing is rarely built with such a sophisticated design. Dark grey concrete etched with abstracted roses gives its cantilevered volumes a luxe texture. Despite looking completely modern, there are references to the past. The staggered facade is reminiscent of a sloped street of NYC row houses, while the sporadically spaced windows recall those that dot across brick apartment towers. Inside is the Sugar Hill Children's Museum of Art & Storytelling, dedicated to nurturing the creative spirit of underserved youth. A decade on from its completion, it remains exciting to see a chance being taken on something unabashedly bold that is not reserved for the elite.

898 St Nicholas Avenue, New York, NY 10032
Nearest subway: 155th Street (C)
Access: The Sugar Hill Children's Museum of Art
& Storytelling is open to the public
sugarhillmuseum.org

Adjaye Associates (2015)

58

SYLVAN TERRACE

Charming portal to the past

Walk up the staircase between the stone walls on St Nicholas Avenue below 161st Street, and you'll be transported back in time. Twenty nearly identical wood-framed townhouses are preserved just as they were in the 19th century. At the end of the block is the 1765 Morris–Jumel Mansion, the oldest surviving house in Manhattan; this Belgian block cobblestone road was once its carriage path. Over the decades, the townhouses fell into disrepair and were covered with stucco and aluminium siding. (Peek at their backs through the fence to see evidence of these alterations.) Restoration in the early 1980s revived them with a matching colour scheme in lively green, yellow and brown.

Sylvan Terrace, New York, NY 10032
Nearest subway: 163rd Street–Amsterdam Avenue (C)
Access: Private homes, street access only

Gilbert Robinson Jr (1882–83)

59

DYCKMAN FARMHOUSE MUSEUM

A reminder of Manhattan's agrarian past

Upper Manhattan remained rural into the early 20th century, even when tenements and skyscrapers were rising downtown. This is now Manhattan's last surviving Dutch Colonial farmhouse. The Dyckman family's first farm was destroyed in the American Revolution and rebuilt from brick, fieldstone and wood around 1784. Although hemmed in by apartment buildings and facing a commercial strip, the two-storey house appears much as it did then, with broad porches and a sloped roof. It was donated to the city in 1916 and has been a historic institution ever since, with recent programming recognising the enslaved people who lived here. Its freely accessible garden is an especially lovely urban respite.

4881 Broadway, New York, NY 10034
Nearest subway: Inwood–207th Street (A)
Access: Garden access free; ticketed museum
admission and tours
dyckmanfarmhouse.org

William Dyckman (ca. 1784)

60

TRACEY TOWERS

Brutalist columns of concrete

Architect Paul Rudolph saw the future of cities as megastructures. One of his most astounding and terrifying ideas was to build a two-mile-long complex that would stack apartments over a Manhattan expressway. These twin residential towers are more subdued but still imposingly modernist against the flat Bronx skyline. Ribbed concrete bricks curve away from windows and balconies, an undulating shape that contrasts with the angular forms of other affordable housing projects. Rudolph made that sculptural rough concrete a signature of his work. Some may find these buildings more fortress than home, yet they demonstrate that even masses of low-cost prefabricated materials like concrete can be used with creativity.

20 & 40 West Mosholu Parkway South,
Bronx, NY 10468
Nearest subway: Mosholu Parkway (4)
Access: Closed to the public, view from the street

Paul Rudolph (1972)

61

BRONX COMMUNITY COLLEGE: GOULD MEMORIAL LIBRARY

The crown of a college on a hill

Bronx Community College quietly has some of NYC's best architecture, including several Brutalist structures by Marcel Breuer. When designing a library for what was then New York University's uptown campus, Stanford White was inspired by a wonder of the Classical world: Rome's Pantheon. Like the Pantheon, the dome of his Beaux-Arts temple of knowledge has an oculus. It shines down from 70 feet into a circular reading room presided over by green marble columns. White's other works, like the Washington Square Arch (no.16), may be better known, but many contend that this is his greatest building. After a late 20th-century deterioration, a recent reconstruction of its dome has restored some of its magnificence.

2060 Sedgwick Avenue, Bronx, NY 10453
Nearest subway: 183rd Street (4)
Access: Contact the college for current accessibility
bcc.cuny.edu

Stanford White (1900)

LIBRARY OF NEW YORK UNIVERSITY MDCCC

62

THE HIGH BRIDGE

NYC's oldest surviving bridge

By the late 18th century, it was clear that New York needed ample clean water to support its growing metropolis. The solution was the incredible gravity-powered system known as the Croton Aqueduct that brought water down from upstate. Its showpiece as it entered the city was the Roman-inspired High Bridge, a 1,450-foot link between Manhattan and the Bronx. Its fashionable promenade hid a water pipe within. A 20th-century decline of the waterfront led to it being closed to public access in the 1970s. Spurred by local interest, a rehabilitation culminated in its 2015 reopening to pedestrians and cyclists, and now this wonder of engineering can once again be appreciated from 138 feet in the air.

Harlem River between the Bronx and Manhattan
Nearest subways: Bronx side, 170th Street (4);
Manhattan side, 168th Street (A/C/1)
Access: Open daily, 7am–10pm
nycgovparks.org

John B. Jervis (1848)

63

HUNTERS POINT LIBRARY

A flawed gem on the waterfront

So many years of planning went into this branch of the Queens Public Library, yet when it finally opened, there was immediate criticism of its accessibility issues. Three levels of its fiction shelves could only be reached by stairs. Lawsuits quickly followed. The building received critical acclaim, however, for its design, where sculpted walls are clad in bamboo and illuminated by the massive windows that slash through its concrete exterior. These look out to the East River waterfront, which before its recent rapid development was industrial. Major renovations are now planned to address its issues, so this enchanting building for books and community can actually be a place for all.

47-40 Center Boulevard, Long Island City, NY 11109
Nearest subway: Vernon Boulevard–Jackson Avenue (7)
Access: Open to the public
queenslibrary.org

Steven Holl Architects (2019)

64

TWA FLIGHT CENTER

Aviation glamour restored

Ever since this 1960s terminal was converted into a hotel in 2019, long delays and stopovers at John F. Kennedy International Airport have had the perfect antidote. Cocktails are served below the cantilevered bridge of its curvaceous lobby; the futuristic 'flight tubes' that once led passengers to aircraft now connect to guest rooms. It all harks back to the post-war optimism of the Jet Age, when airlines had their own terminals. TWA red and white are colours here throughout. Although Finnish–American architect Eero Saarinen may be more famous for designing St Louis's Gateway Arch, this is his most soaring achievement. He expressed the miracle of flight itself in the swooping concrete.

1 Idlewild Drive, Queens, NY 11430
Nearest subway: AirTrain at Terminal 5
Access: Apart from guest rooms, most areas are accessible;
guided tours must be booked in advance
twahotel.com

Eero Saarinen and Associates (1962)

65
BROOKLYN BRIDGE

From shore to shore with stone and steel

As an act of engineering, the Brooklyn Bridge is a marvel. It was the world's longest suspension bridge when it opened, and long before skyscrapers crowded Manhattan, its monumentality announced that this was a modern city that would become a metropolis. Its two granite towers, from which huge cables descend, rise 278 feet out of the water. Each has a pair of airy Gothic Revival pointed arches, under which thousands of pedestrians, bikes and cars pass every day. Most tourists gather in hordes on the shore of Brooklyn Bridge Park to view it at sunset. It's better to set your alarm for sunrise and walk across the bridge itself, witnessing the city come alive in the rosy light.

East River between Manhattan and Brooklyn
Nearest subways: Brooklyn side, High Street (A/C);
Manhattan side, Brooklyn Bridge–City Hall/Chambers
Street (4/5/6/J/Z)
Access: Open to the public

John Roebling (1883)

66

KINGS THEATRE

Movie palace's second act

One of the five Loew's Wonder Theatres built in the New York area, this venue recalls when seeing a movie was an event. Versailles and the Opéra Garnier in Paris inspired its opulent 1920s decor. After closing in 1977, it was abandoned, decaying from neglect and vandalism as its roof caved and water got in. All seemed lost until its restoration as a stunning concert venue, opening in 2015. The meticulous revival is now part of the show. Birds and flora adorn the terracotta facade; the auditorium's 50,000-square-foot ceiling is plastered with ornamentation. See a show or book a historic building tour to discover touches like the walnut panelling accents on the walls and the Art Deco chandeliers that glow in the lobby.

1027 Flatbush Avenue, Brooklyn, NY 11226
Nearest subway: Beverly Road (Q)
Access: Paid entry to events and building tours
kingstheatre.com

*Rapp & Rapp (1929); Martinez+Johnson Architecture,
EverGreene Architectural Arts and Gilbane (2015)*

67

GREEN-WOOD CEMETERY ARCH

Ornate entrance to the empire of the dead

Visiting a New York cemetery did not used to be an event. The colonial churchyards were grim and sombre affairs, with tightly packed graves marked with headstones topped by winged skulls. When what's known as the rural cemetery movement took off in the 19th century, burials moved to garden-like spaces, and the architecture of mourning changed to emphasise death as a transition to a beautiful afterlife. This grand Gothic Revival gateway reinforces that idea, announcing to visitors that they have entered a necropolis, a city of the departed. Made from brownstone and resembling the front of a cathedral, its bell tower is home to a chattering flock of green monk parakeets.

25th Street and Fifth Avenue, Brooklyn, NY 11232
Nearest subway: 25th Street (R)
Access: Open daily, check seasonal hours online
green-wood.com

Richard Upjohn and Son (1865)

68
WYCKOFF HOUSE

The great old one

The steeply sloped roof and wood shingles make this Dutch Colonial farmhouse stand out as a ghost of another time. It faces the obliterated Canarsie Lane, a former road that linked colonial settlements and had earlier history as a Lenape hunting path. Although expanded by the Wyckoff family over the years, its original one-room house dates to around 1652, making it New York's oldest structure. Before the 1664 English takeover, this was New Amsterdam. In the centuries before its neighbours were car washes and repair shops, enslaved and free Black people and immigrants farmed the surrounding land. The house's programming today focuses as much on this diverse heritage as on the historic architecture itself, such as festivals of Caribbean culture.

5816 Clarendon Road, Brooklyn, NY 11203
Nearest subway: Canarsie–Rockaway Parkway (L)
Access: Schedule of public house tours and events is online
wyckoffmuseum.org

Unknown (ca. 1652)

69

WEEKSVILLE HERITAGE CENTER

Remnants of a free Black town

Three wooden-framed structures known as the Hunterfly Road Houses are facing a street that no longer exists. It was a thoroughfare in one of the country's largest free Black communities that predated the American Civil War. These are the only physical reminders that Weeksville – founded in 1838 on land acquired by the formerly enslaved James Weeks – was here. It was thought that nothing was left following urban renewal and the expansion of the adjacent neighbourhoods, until local historians identified the buildings in 1968. The sturdiness of the homes, with their parlours and porches, reflects the solidity of the community that was a haven for many fleeing slavery in the South.

158 Buffalo Avenue, Brooklyn, NY 11213
Nearest subway: Ralph Avenue (C)
Access: Free access during open hours; guided
tours are listed online
weeksvillesociety.org

Built from 1840 to 1880

70

PARK SLOPE HISTORIC DISTRICT

NYC's largest landmarked neighbourhood

When people think of Brooklyn, they often envision Park Slope: streets lined with trees and symmetrical rows of brownstones. Before it was the quintessential borough neighbourhood, it was rural, rapidly developing after the establishment of Prospect Park in 1867, the opening of the Brooklyn Bridge (no.65) in 1883 and the consolidation of the city of Brooklyn into New York City in 1898. Stroll along its broad streets at the park, and notice how the most extravagant mansions border the green space. Further down is block after block of smart row houses. Developers designed whole sections of homes in the late 19th into the early 20th century with a uniform appearance – with styles ranging from Queen Anne to Romanesque – cashing in on Brooklyn becoming the trendy place to live.

Roughly bordered by Sixth Avenue, Flatbush Avenue,
Prospect Park West, and 14th Street
Nearest subway: Grand Army Plaza (2/3)
Access: Public access on the streets, most buildings private

Various (between 1862 and 1920)

71

BATTERY WEED

Vestige of a city on the frontlines

The first American wars were fought along the shores of New York. Forts lining the waterways date back to the Revolutionary era, anticipating an attack by sea. Several still stand, with the massive Battery Weed being one of the most architecturally incredible. It faces the Narrows, the gateway for ships arriving from the Atlantic. Solid slabs of granite form walls six feet thick; four tiers of arcades hold up to 116 cannons. It was completed during the Civil War and later renamed for New Yorker Stephen Weed, who was killed at Gettysburg. It is part of the Fort Wadsworth military installation, and you can explore its fortifications and take in panoramic harbour views.

N Weed Road, Staten Island, NY 10305
Nearest subway: None; bus service available
Access: Accessible as part of the Gateway
National Recreation Area
nps.gov/gate/index.htm

Joseph G. Totten (1861)

IMAGE CREDITS

Page 2 © Adam Goldberg; page 4 © Nico De Pasquale Photography; page 6 © Eyetronic; page 7 © Chuck Choi; page 8 © Iwan Baan; page 9 © Ed Reeve; Oculus first image © George Clerk, second image © Alexander / Adobe Stock; One World Trade Center & 9/11 Memorial first image © James Ewing, second image © Andrews Garcia; 41 Cooper Square © Iwan Baan; Whitney Museum of American Art © Whitney Museum of American Art; Woolworth Building © Robert Harding; Jefferson Market Library © Andrew Prokos; Trinity Church © Colin Winterbottom; SoHo–Cast Iron Historic District © Joshua White – Judd Foundation Archives. Image © Judd Foundation; 5 Beekman Street © Björn Wallander / OTTO; Tenement Museum © Tenement Museum; Washington Square Arch © Pawel Gaul; Bayard–Condict Building © James Caufield; David N. Dinkins Municipal Building © Eric Laudonien; Eldridge Street Synagogue © Barbara Ash; Silver Towers © Mark Wickens; National Maritime Union Building © Chris Cooper; Perelman Performing Arts Center © Iwan Baan; Spring Street Salt Shed © Chuck Choi; New Museum © Dean Drake, courtesy of New Museum; One Wall Street © One Wall Street; Saint Nicholas Greek Orthodox Church © Alan Karchmer; Statue of Liberty © Patrick Gross; Hearst Tower © Chuck Choi / OTTO; Lever House Lucas Blair Simpson © SOM; Chrysler Building © Ozgurdonmaz; Empire State Building © West End 61; General Electric Building first image © Petr Svarc, second image © Andy Kazie; Helmsley Building © Alexander Severin; Flatiron Building © Lazy Llama; The High Line © Bailey-Cooper Photography; Ford Foundation Center for Social Justice © Garrett Rowland; Grand Central Terminal first image © C Mart 7327, second image © Bailey-Cooper Photography; New York Public Library © Max Touhey; Radio City Music Hall © Brian Jannsen; Hotel Chelsea © Francois Roux; The Morgan Library & Museum first image © Brett Beyer, second image © Graham Haber; Seagram Building © Pavel Tochinsky; American Radiator Building © Pavel Bendov; Modulightor Building © Annie Schlechter; Rockefeller Center © David Shankbone; 432 Park Avenue Courtesy Rafael Viñoly Architects, © Halkin Mason; Franklin D. Roosevelt Four Freedoms Park © Iwan Baan; 550 Madison Avenue © Alan Schien; Steinway Tower © Michael Lee; Lincoln Center for the Performing Arts © Eileen_10; The Arches of Central Park © Freeman; Gilder Center © Iwan Baan; Solomon R. Guggenheim Museum first image © Library of Congress, second image © Carol M. Highsmith; Park Avenue Armory © James Ewing; Breuer Building © Max Touhey; Studio Museum in Harlem © Albert Vecerka; Sugar Hill Development © Ed Reeve; Sylvan Terrace © Gloria Kilbourne; Dyckman Farmhouse Museum © Dyckman Farmhouse Museu; Tracey Towers © Darren Bradley / OTTO; Bronx Community College: Gould Memorial Library first and second images © Elizabeth Lidel, third image © Faith Ergun; The High Bridge © Wirestock Inc.; Hunters Point Library © Paul Warchol; TWA Flight Center © Max Touhey; Brooklyn Bridge first image © Sereda Tomas, second image © Diana Robinson; Kings Theatre © Kenneth Grant; Green-Wood Cemetery Arch © Roy Rochlin; Wyckoff House © Andrew Carrotflower; Weeksville Heritage Center © Matthew Kiernan; Park Slope Historic District © Francis Roux; Battery Weed © Kenneth Grant.

An Opinionated Guide to New York Architecture
First edition, first printing

Published in 2026 by Hoxton Mini Press, London.
Copyright © Hoxton Mini Press 2026. All rights reserved.
Text © Allison C. Meier 2026

Text by Allison C. Meier
Editing by Kate Overy
Production design by Dom Grant
Production control by David Brimble
Proofreading by Dean Drake
Editorial support by Richard Enright

With thanks to Matthew Young for
initial series design.

Please note: we recommend checking the
websites listed for each entry before you
visit for the latest information on price,
opening times and pre-booking
requirements.

Thank you to all of the individuals and
institutions who have provided images
and arranged permissions. While every
effort has been made to trace the present
copyright holders we apologise in advance
for any unintentional omission or error,
and would be pleased to insert the
appropriate acknowledgement in any
subsequent edition.

A CIP catalogue record for this book is
available from the British Library.

ISBN: 978-1-917719-17-9

Printed and bound by OZGraf, Poland

Manufacturer: Hoxton Mini Press, 104
Northside Studios, 16–29 Andrews Road,
London E8 4QF, UK
www.hoxtonminipress.com

Represented by: Authorised Rep
Compliance Ltd., Ground Floor, 71 Lower
Baggot Street, Dublin DO2 P593, Ireland
www.arccompliance.com

Hoxton Mini Press is an environmen-
tally conscious publisher, committed
to offsetting our carbon footprint.
This book is 100 per cent carbon
compensated, with offset purchased
from Stand For Trees.

Every time you order from our website, we
plant a tree: www.hoxtonminipress.com

Selected opinionated guides in the series:
For more go to www.hoxtonminipress.com

ABOUT HOXTON
MINI PRESS

Hoxton Mini Press is a small indie publisher based in east London. We make beautiful books with a dedication to sustainable production and great photography.

When we started the company, people told us print was dead; we wanted to prove them wrong. Books are no longer just about information, but objects to collect and own.

We promise three things. Firstly, nothing in this guidebook is sponsored; it's our own independent opinion. Secondly, our books are 100 per cent carbon compensated with printing, paper and transport fully offset. And finally, everything is researched, edited and written by humans, not AI.